Four Minute Essays

By

Dr. Frank Crane

Volume IV

Wm. H. Wise & Co., Inc.
New York   Chicago

TABLE OF CONTENTS

4   TABLE OF CONTENTS

GREAT LOVE AND MUCH SERVICE

IT is the commonest things in the world
that most need definition.

There are certain vital subjects the mind
handles every day, indeed must handle because they are as essential to thought as
bread and water to the body; and by much
handling these subjects become smooth as
old coins. Once in a while it is well to ex-
amine them minutely to see what "image
and superscription" is thereon.

Nothing is more constantly spoken of
than happiness. It is the end of religion,
the object of philosophy, the dream of the
wretched, the quest of the whole world.

BUT WHAT IS IT?

Suppose we ask ourselves that? And suppose we patiently and honestly try to find an answer? If we discover what happiness is, or at least what it means to us, we have gone a long way toward grasping happiness, the thing itself.

And just to stimulate your inquiry allow me to hand to you a definition I read the other day, I know not where. It is this:

HAPPINESS IS GREAT LOVE AND MUCH SERVICE.

If you will look about carefully among the people you know, not neglecting yourself, you will discover that not one of them is happy that does not love. Furthermore that all of them are happy in proportion as they love.

Happiness is the perfume of the rose of love, the light shining from the candle of love, the sound from the bells of love.

You can get a certain something that resembles happiness from the gratification of desire, from eating, drinking, playing, and the like. But it all has in itself the seed of boredom. You get SATED from satisfying appetite; but in the happiness that comes from love is no satiety.

What is true of love is equally true of service; because to love is to serve.

Search again among the people you know, and note that they are happy in proportion as they serve.

The great mass of men and women are reasonably content because they are at work.

They often complain of their work. They even call labor a curse. But they would be miserable without it.

They dream of a life of idleness and self-indulgence, and many imagine that is heaven. It is not. It is hell.

This world was made for lovers and for servants.

If any one's heart is full of love, and his hand full of service, he has no morbid "problems." He has solved the riddle of life.

THE CHRYSANTHEMUM

AFTER the roses have fallen and their leaves lie a dawn-tinted carpet around the shivering bush; after the warmth-loving heliotrope and sunflower and petunia have smiled up at their cooling lover, the sun, and died; after the Herod frost has stabbed all the little summer-innocents of the garden, and they have dropped their heads forever, then comes the splendid chrysanthemum, the last flaunting banner of the flower army retreating before the enemy of all life—the cold.

Its beauty is akin to its season. For its colors are not strong and crying, but touched with a pensive shade; not fresh pinks and hot scarlets, but a pink softened and a red diluted; not the color of the sun, but that of the moon, and of the haze upon morning waters.

Chrysanthemum colors are as characteristic as nasturtium colors; they are of all kinds, yet with a pervading quality. The same subdued thoughtfulness runs through all. There are straw colors and cream, sulphur and tarnished gold, saffron and orange and salmon, colors of old rose and violet, magenta and nut brown, but all steeped in mystery.

It is the flower of melancholy, notwithstanding its assertive size and splendor. It is the flower that flourishes on All Souls' Day, the Day of the Dead.

It is an immigrant, as the people of America are immigrants. But while they come from Europe, the chrysanthemum comes from the Levant. In China long ago Confucius celebrated its "golden glory." It was adopted by the Japanese, who made the little beggar-flower of the roadside to be the gorgeous emblem of chivalry, for princes of the blood only. They stamped its image upon their ancient moneys, upon the seal of the mikado, upon the sabre-hilts of the soldiers of the guard.

The Japanese have employed the chrysanthemum, together with the cherry blossom, the bamboo, and the nenuphar as the standard figures of their ingenious decorative art.

The chrysanthemum is one of the most striking examples of what man can do with the simple products of nature. The timid, small, yellow flower that came to us from overseas has become fantastic, monstrous, fulsome, and bold. It has perked up its petals "like quills upon the fretful porcupine," rolled them around like serpents, crimped them as ladies do their hair. Little by little the horticulturists have made a queen of this Cophetua blossom.

There is nothing that so crashes upon one's sense of beauty, that so comes over one's spirit like a blare of trumpets, as a massed display of these royal flowers.

The chrysanthemum is summer's swan-song, full of elegiac majesty; it is the summer's last caress, sweet as the sweetness of that one more kiss we place upon the lips of the beloved who are about to die.

COMMON SENSE

COMMON SENSE is the sense, or wisdom, which the mind absorbs from all the common and ordinary things of life. It is more reliable than any wisdom drawn from uncommon things. For what keeps happening has more of the juice of the universe in it than the thing that happens once in a while.

Most things that are plain, and that we know thoroughly, are those things that we have observed over and over again; as repetition is the mother of certainty. A mysterious event, or a miracle, is simply something that happens only once. If there were a volcanic eruption every day at 6 a. m., we should pay no more attention to it than to a sunrise.

Common Sense is very complex, and unconscious of itself. "Book learning," and all expert and professional and unusual knowledge, is simple, and understands itself perfectly. Hence the so-called learned men, and those who have mastered some craft, are as a rule quite sure they know something. The shrewd student of life, the man who, like Lincoln, has his force in the Common Sense he has amassed, is, on the contrary, inclined to doubt if he knows anything.

By and by, in the course of centuries, even if not of years, or months, Common Sense becomes the judge and jury of every science, every religion, every art, every government. No system or institution will stand unless it will adjust itself to the slow, silent, merciless criticism of Common Sense.

MANNERS

Y OUR manner has a deal to do with your
success.

Your manners are the printed page on
which people read of what you are inside.

So what's the use of being grand and
noble in your thought, intent, and purpose
if the whole story is twisted, botched, and
lied about by your way of expressing yourself?

People are usually very sensitive, very
stupid, and very silly on the matter of im-
proving their ways. They resent it when
they are told to talk differently, to sit, walk,
or stand in a better style.

You are apt to say: "I am what I am. If

people don't like me I can't help it. I am
as God made me."

But you are not. You are as circumstances, environment, and your own ignorance
have spoiled you.

If you have a friend—an enemy is even
better—who dares tell you the truth, go to
him, and listen, and think over what he says.

When any one criticizes you, or when you
hear something disagreeable said of you,
don't repel it with anger, but study over it,
find out if it has a basis of truth, and improve yourself. Don't defend; reform.

Why should you let an unfortunate man-
nerism cling to you all your life, just because
you are too lazy or too proud to rid yourself
of it?

Do you walk lumberingly? Do you sit
awkwardly? Have you got into the way of
scowling habitually? Is your voice harsh

and unpleasant, or loud, or shrill? Do you mumble your words?

You can change all these things and re-move the disagreeable spot that is hurting you more than any one else if (1) you will acknowledge and see your weakness, and (2) if you will steadily practise to overcome.

Don't be a conceited fool. Don't make your objectionable qualities a part of your personality, which you feel called on always to defend.

One way to success is to get the manner of success.

Find some one whom you admire, some one who has poise and dignity and ease and is just about the sort of person you wish you were. Study him. Imitate him. Copy his little ways.

It's these little things that count. It makes a lot of difference how you speak, whether your words are coarse, inaccurate, and provincial or not.

Have courage to quit slouching, to learn how to sit correctly, to eat like a person of breeding, to quit screwing your mouth about, and laughing like a horse, and asking the price of your host's dishes, and blowing your nose like a trumpet, and using such negroid words as "humanitarian" and "enthuse" and all such things

Usually it is carelessness more than ignorance.

NEWS FROM THE SHENANDOAH

HAVE you heard the great news from the Shenandoah Valley? I have just been down there and will tell it you.

Amazing, shattering, glorious news. I was eye-witness and saw it all from a car window riding from Hagerstown to Winchester on the Cumberland Railway. Yes, I actually saw the great spring drive. Life, or rather the myriad lives, came over the Blue Ridge, swept all before them, and conquered every hill and hollow with rampant beauty.

The meadow lands were painted deep with the richest, freshest, liveliest green imaginable, that greenness which is the very blood of God. And all about were scattered fruit-trees, salvos of beauty, puffs of white and pink. Here and there ploughed strips of land, a bright rich brown, great checkered squares bespeaking hidden seeds and future plenty.

It was not raining, but sky and air were full of potential rain, the spirit of rain hovered everywhere, and made every living thing laugh with health.

Suddenly, as we rounded a hill, a little orchard of peach-trees burst on my sight, an inconceivably gorgeous rosy mass of loveliness, delicate and appealing as a young girl stepping from childhood into love time.

Over in the woods was some pyramidal tree-shape of light greenish yellow, here and there other trees of cherry red, and still others, innumerable others, of fluffy popcorn white.

One stream we passed, guarded it was on both sides by trees whose winter nudity was more revealed than concealed by the thin gauze of hazy leafage, as if they were young goddesses stepping down in the sanctity of their pure self-revelation to the water's edge.

Youth everywhere. Genetic force. Promises crowding the air. An intoxicating hope inbreathing all things. Loveliness calling for love.

Nature had unlocked at last and revealed her secret. I had surprised the heart of things. It was unutterably beautiful.

And all about at the horizon the mountains, indistinct, swathed in mist, bluish gray, as dim and mysterious death surrounds life (perhaps as tenderly good and gracious as life), or as the mountains of the past and of the future are forever at the horizon of the present.

News from the Shenandoah! The earth is young! Spring is here! Wake up, cheer up, old hearts!

> "God's in His heaven,
> All's right with the world!"

CEILINGS

MAN gained much but lost something when he exchanged the sky for the ceiling.

Civilization is a great gain. It is also the mother of infinite diseases.

It is the house that is doing more than fire-water to exterminate the red man.

Jesus and Buddha taught under the sky; creeds were made under ceilings.

The sky breeds universality; the ceiling provincialism.

It is good for a man to spend some part of every day under the sky, that mayhap a little of it may sink into his soul.

It is good for him also to go out often in the night, for the stars have a most vital message, as it is written, "There is no speech nor language where their voice is not heard."

Our souls are not skyey enough.

Beneath the sky our sins are simple and human.

The devil must live in a house somewhere with a low ceiling. God lives in the sky.

The ideal school would be where there is a teacher wise enough to wander with the children in the woods and lead out their minds in self-expression.

The ideal church would hold its meetings in the sunshine, where the light of day could dissolve superstition, and the free wind drive away the foul gases of sectarian pride.

We have developed a race of men afraid of the sky. Our business is transacted, our books are written, our songs are sung, our pictures are painted, our lutes are twanged, our food is eaten, our theatres are held, our loves are made, our dreams are dreamt, under ceilings.

Hence they are, as the painters say, "hot and foxy."

On all we do is the mark of artificiality, a certain mediocrity and cheapness, an absence of that large freedom, that calm majesty, that should characterize this animal, man, in whom dwells divinity.

The curse of all thought is provincialism, which is the breath of ceilings. From our narrowness come all our woes. If we had the sky-spirit, and sensed the universal, we should have no more clashing egotisms, hot partisanships, mad patriotisms, insane race hates, stubborn feuds, nor any of the hell-brood of class.

Class, of all kinds, is a ceiling-bred folly.

Humanity, democracy, universal brotherhood, and the one God—these are of the sky.

CREATURE OR CREATOR?

ARE you Creature or Creator?
Says Ernest Crosby:

"Where are the cowards who bow down
to environment—
Who think they are made of what they
eat?
I am not wax. I am energy.
I have my ideas to work out, and the
universe is given me for raw material.
I am a vortex launched in chaos to suck
it into shape."

It all depends upon your point of view.
You can be either clay or potter, the ball or
the pitcher, a thing or a god.

Why do you talk of being the victim of

circumstances? You can just as well be the master of circumstances.

I am no puppet of fate. I am secretly in partnership with fate.

Whatever else He may be, God is a spirit. And I am also a spirit.

He is not an image of stone. Neither am I a mere organism of flesh.

He leads the stars, informs the lily, guides the wayward river, moulds the rain-drop, turns on the aurora, and drives the chariot of the sun.

I, who am His kin, am also no clod.

I find a way. I create opportunity. I yoke the winds to my sails and the steam to my cylinders.

I speak to bricks and they fall in by platoons and become my walls.

I gesture to electricity, and it lights my house, draws my roaring express-train, and carries my words in a flash across continents and under oceans.

I can also make tears and laughter. I can darken hearts with pain and light them with joy.

I can discourage the eager boy and soil the clean soul of the girl. I can sow doubt, discord, discontent. I can be as efficient in evil as the devil.

I have no excuse. If I have got drunk it was I who swallowed the stuff. I must pay the debts of my madness.

If I have failed, seek no further. It is I who am to blame. For there is to me no failure anywhere in the world that counts, except the failure within my soul.

No man, no woman can defile me. The soul's nest is never fouled save by itself.

And if I have succeeded, give me the credit and not another, nor luck, nor happenings.

For success is a spiritual somewhat. Even when it comes to the inward failure he cannot hold it. It falls from his hands.

I take my reward. I take my punishment. Both are mine.

I am no horse. No one rides me and pulls my bridle. I am the rider.

I can go to hell if I want to. I can go to heaven if I prefer.

I am a free spirit. All around me and within me flows the Universal Spirit. He is Creator. So am I. We work together.

If I have poise and peace and prosperity it is due to us, to our creative partnership.

I am no Creature. I am a co-Creator.

THE KINSHIP OF FRAILTY

EVERY once in a while you read of some great man or some good man that he was never subject to strong passions, that he never fell into the tantrums nor spoke in a loud voice nor otherwise fought or nearly fought. All very well; but would life be very interesting with one of these superior beings? And do they themselves not miss something which after all is the most stirring, if not the best, part of the story? There is something to be said in favor of anger, petulance, sulks, quarrels, and blues, also fights. They are the high lights. They are the brilliant reds and yellows of life. Of course, too much of them smacks of vulgarity. But who wants his days all drab?

These strong tempers we are supposed to inherit from our savage ancestors. They belong to our "lower nature." But is it not along the substratum of our lower selves that we are most akin? We are animals, after all; why turn up our noses at the fact? Is not a deal of this super-spirituality largely streaked with affectation? As a matter of fact, one touch of Flesh makes the whole world kin.

Washington came within an inch of being last forever in "the hearts of his countrymen"; it was his little swearing episode that saved him. The jagged words the Nazarene hurled at the Pharisees, and his chasing the money-changers from the Temple, link him strongly to our humanity. The heroes of Homer and Aristotle, the men of ruder times than ours, who let themselves go in towering emotions, seem to have lent a richer color

to life than our unmoved modern Great
Ones, who sit serene at mahogany tables and
crush their victims with Money.—Of course,
it is naughty to flare up: but humanity is
not Putty—not yet. The most moral man is
the completest man; and needs Fire, too.

FEAR OF GREATNESS

DON'T be afraid of your generous emotions.

The worst fear is the fear to be too great.

The meanest satisfaction is to be content in being like others.

If you trust a friend, trust him unto death. Of course you may be deceived in him. But better be humiliated by betrayal than be incapable of perfect faith.

If you love your wife, love loyally utterly. She may not appreciate it. But better be unappreciated than to miss the joy of perfect self-giving.

Don't be too afraid of casting your pearls before swine. Better that than to hoard your pearls. And Jesus, who said it, did cast His pearls before many swine.

Don't be afraid to forgive. The object of your forgiveness may be unworthy, but that cannot mar the fineness of your pardon.

Don't be afraid to show yourself friendly, for only so you show yourself worth friendship.

Don't be afraid to believe in goodness. Better that evil should come as a shock than that you should have trusted in it.

Don't be afraid of being too kind. "In this world," says Marivaux, "one must be a little too kind to be kind enough."

MY CASTLE

I WISH you could see my castle. It is a wonderful place.

It is old, so old, that the historians do not know when it was built. A place is not really a home unless it be old. One might as well be in a hotel as in a new house.

It has grown; that is more accurate than to say it was built.

Each generation had added to or taken from it, or altered it to suit.

It rises from the edge of a river. From the door you can step into a boat. A green sward on the other side slopes down to a lake. In the distance is the sea. Back to the north is a high mountain on which the

snow lingers until June, making of the peak
a white needle that is silver and glass and
gold in the evening sun. A forest of ancient trees is in my park.

Entering my house you find yourself in
a broad hall that leads to a central court
where there are palms and a fountain and
rose-trees.

The family room is very large, as spacious
as a banquet-hall. At one end is a fireplace
great enough to burn full-length cord-wood.
Beside it are wide leathern seats. The ceiling is of oak and heavily beamed. Wide
windows on all sides open down to the floor.

All the wall space throughout the castle
is occupied with bookshelves. The house
is one huge library. All the great books in
the world are there. I have them all bound
in uniform red limp leather, with my book-
plate in gilt on each.

I have a stenographer who speaks ten languages and takes dictation as rapidly as I can give it. She has never made a mistake.

My study is full of light. A wood-fire crackles cheerily while I work. And every morning fresh roses or lilies or other soft-breathed flowers are on my desk.

There are twenty guest-chambers, and the castle is always full of company. The most clever, learned, and intelligent men and women of the whole world come to visit me.

There are also a bevy of young people of ginger-beer age, popping with enthusiasm, ever with me. I cannot do without them. In my dozen automobiles they make daily excursions round about.

Ships from the Orient can sail up the river to my door; and they bring strange stuffs and woods and spices, and amuse us with their different manners and speech.

It is always tempered summer where I live. The smell of oranges, of tamarinds, and of flowers is in the air continually.

I have a treasurer who supplies me with all the money I need, a secretary who attends to my correspondence, a tailor who looks after my clothing, a factor who manages the castle and estate, a chef who is a past master in cooking, a physician who attends to the health of all, a devout man who has taken holy orders in Mohammedanism, Buddhism, and Christianity, and who therefore keeps us supplied with juicy argument, a fool who amuses us when we are bored, and a wife who looks after my immortal soul.

Alas! I am afraid you can never find this place, much as I should love to have you come and see me.

For my castle is in Spain.

LIFE A TIGHT-ROPE WALK

THE path of life is a narrow ridge between two insanities.

Living a sane, normal, healthy life is like walking the tight-rope.

When he looks over to one side, a man see chasms, sickening depths, the terrifying unknown. On the other side is the same.

It is a very proper expression we use when we say of a man that he is "unbalanced." Sanity is simply equilibrium.

How few people can gaze squarely into the emptiness of Death, that vast bottomless pit, and not feel panic! As few as they who can climb peaks, steeples, and masts, and keep their head.

How few people can regard God, the overpowering infinite, and not clutch at some idol, as a man falling down a precipice grasps at roots and vines! We must, for our weakness, replace the dazzling mystery of God by some little, comfortable, painted superstition. A bit of hocus-pocus, a sign, a formula, a venerable and empty symbol— anything is better than the shattering reality! We cherish our petty artificial certainties, our plaster credences, because we cannot understand how the truest of all truths may be an Uncertainty. No; that way madness lies, except for a few.

Let us pray for Head, for poise, for the sound stomach, and solid brain, and strong-pounding heart, so that we can walk dizzy edges happily, feel easy in the dark, look fearlessly into the gulfs that pull weaker men, kiss Death sweetly on the mouth when

our call comes, and breast the thunders of
Afterwards unafraid. Let no vertigo rob
us of God.

HOW TO READ THE BIBLE

I HAVE no particular creed I want you to swallow, and no particular church I want you to join. I have no intention to convert you, and don't even aim to "do you good."

Still, a friendly hint on how to read the Bible may interest you.

You may read the Bible from moral motives, or merely as literature. In the one case you may find it a very puzzling book, and in the other very antique, unless you remember one thing.

The one thing is that the Bible is an Oriental book.

Unless you keep that in mind you are

pretty sure to miss its meaning. Some of
the most absurd vagaries have arisen by for-
getting it, and by treating the Bible as a
Western book.

The oriental mind differs from ours
chiefly in this, that it is essentially poetic.
Eastern peoples have always thought, spoken, and written poetry. They cannot write
prose when they try.

Poetry does not speak plainly. It hints,
symbolizes; touches facts not with a rough,
firm grasp, but evasively; loves riddles, dark
sayings, and apparent contradictions.

It functions in parables and paradoxes.

The western mind is prosaic. It plods,
builds, reasons.

To get to the top of the mountain, the
occidental cuts logical steps in the rocks; the
oriental flies.

In moral subjects and religious the eastern mind is the more skilful, as such matters are better divined than argued.

Forget not, therefore, that there is hardly a line of your Bible that is not poetry. The nearest approach to prose is in Paul's writings; yet they also abound in highly poetical passages.

No one had this poetical turn more than the chief figure of the Bible, Jesus.

His parables are pure poetry. His maxims are full of paradox.

It is very unfortunate that our western bent for logic and bald facts led us to use the glowing images of the great Master's poetry as bricks and squared stones wherewith to build up our "systems of truth."

For it is doubtful that truth is a system at all; it is more likely a vision.

Take one illustration: Jesus would teach His disciples the value of humility. Instead of analyzing this virtue, explaining and dissecting it, as a modern professor might do, He removes His coat, girds himself with a towel, and washes His pupils' feet, saying when finished:

"If I, your Master, wash your feet, so ought ye to wash one another's feet."

The advantage of this method of teaching is that it is striking, easily remembered, visual, and interesting.

Common sense prevented His disciples from taking Him literally. They were forced to seek the idea, the sentiment behind it.

Literalism is not truth. It is the foe of truth. "The letter killeth."

You cannot literally obey a poet; you should spiritually obey him; that is, try to appreciate him, to get his point of view, his atmosphere and feeling.

Logic chopping is fatal to all poetry.

THE NEEDLE

WHO made the first needle? Perhaps some clever wife, who pierced the shank of a fine fish-bone to carry a thread of plant fibre or catgut.

Today the Needle is the symbol of civilization; for where you find human beings this side of barbarism you find clothes, and where clothes are there are Needles.

Man is a Tool-Using animal. And the Needle is the commonest and smallest of Tools.

The spider spins his web, the worm his cocoon; the man, by nature naked, weaves his outmost cuticle with this sharp, shining shaft of steel.

I have never seen the Needle factories. Yet they are in my mind's eye huge, many-windowed barracks; and out of them march, day after day, the little soldiers of civilization, in silver-gleaming armor and golden helmets, in companies and regiments, to go to Alaska and Cape Town, to Tokio and New York; to the hands of the mother and the sister; to the morocco case upon the mahogany dressing-table of the darling of wealth, to the workbox of the wife of the people, to the dark rooms of the slaves of the sweatshop, to the pincushion of the bachelor, to the knapsack of the soldier, the bundle of the pioneer, the kit of the sailor. Wherever go the animals called human the little needle dances attendance.

The sword is the instrument of glory; it has been multiplied by inventive genius, transformed into the bullet and the bomb, and made to fall in thunderous hail to magnify the hideous trade of murder.

The pen is the instrument of thought. It has become a type, and its printed words rain thick from the presses in newspapers, magazines, and books.

The knife and spoon have been elaborated into the manifold utensils of the chef who prepares the complicated delicacies for the gourmet.

The rude flint of the ape-man has become the chisel of a Rodin; the coarse hair-clump of the cave-man has grown into the brush of a Millet.

The Needle has developed also. Elias Howe dreamed he was pursued by savages whose spears had holes in them near the point. He awoke to devise the Needle with its eye at the piercing-end. Hence the Sewing-Machine, doing the work of twenty seamstresses, flying with the speed of an electric spark.

It is an automatic, machine-using, power-driven age, with the Needle buzzing attendance.

When Gustave Charpentier, the musician, was presented with the Sword of the Academy by Mimi Pinson, on behalf of the working girls of Paris, whom he had befriended, he replied:

"The sword, the pen, and the brush have won great glory for our country. But has not the Needle also its share? A statue of Mercie, a score of Massenet, a speech of Poincare, each is an ornament to France; but a Paris robe, worn by a Parisienne, is it not also a thing of art, a marvellous art, all the more precious art because enduring but a little time?"

LIFE IS SOMETHING TO DO, NOT SOMETHING TO LEARN

LIFE is hard because it is something to do, not something to learn.

The complaint is very common that life is so mysterious, so complex. Whence come we, whither go, and what does it all mean? As if anybody had any particular right to know its meaning!

Life is not a problem, it is a task. We don't have to understand it, we have to live it. Consequently those simple folk who set themselves about living their days as they come, as happily and usefully as they can, have much saner views about themselves, the world, God, and the devil, than the philos-

ophers and theologians who are cracking
their brains trying to understand.

Why should one make himself unhappy
over what is none of his business? Why I
was brought into the world, why circumstances are as they are around me, why my
disposition is as it is, why I was created a
man and not a woman, why I am living now
and my brother dead, what shall take place
after the phenomenon of death, all these
things by no possibility can I know. They
are none of my affair. Why worry? Nature or God or some invisible power, utterly
outside of my reach and comprehension, is
attending to them.

And I am content. I'm glad I don't have
to help along with destiny.

The man who gets up cheerfully in the
morning and goes to bed reasonably contented every night, and between the two car-

ries out his natural instincts, works hard, plays heartily, thinks honestly, feels strongly and deeply; and who every day tries to do all this a little better; such a man lives.

For life is an art, not a science. It is a trade, not a puzzle. You learn to live as you would learn to lay brick or carve statues or manage a farm. That is to say, you are always learning, and no one can say he is perfect. The complexities and profundities of anything that is to be done are infinite. No one ever knows all there is to be known about ship-building.

But that is no reason why men should not go on building ships, getting a living and some satisfaction out of it, and constructing better and better vessels by practise. And because life as a problem is too much for us, is no reason why life as daily work should not be an enjoyable affair.

But, at bottom, life is not so much a task as it is an opportunity. We are full of forces. Nature means us to operate them. In the functioning of these forces we find pleasure.

It is not enough, however, to say that we are merely to follow our instincts. We have something else besides instincts. We have brains. Reason criticizes and constantly improves the quality of life. Thus the natural forces in us become refined, and produce a pleasure we call higher because it is most lasting and wider in its scope.

Thus, instead of brute lust, we have human love, with all its complexities and tenuous joys; instead of fear of Nature and her powers, we have religion, which is joy in the sum of things; instead of fighting one another for bread and clothing and comforts, we discover how to cooperate one with another and each with all, and so obtain the benefits of organized society and the state.

So with every generation life grows broader and finer. As a problem it is as insoluble now as it was in the days of Job. As a task it is infinitely more varied, interesting, and full.

EXCEPT IT DIE

"THOU fool, that which thou sowest is not quickened except it die."

There is no life that is not prepared by death. Death is the door of life.

A grain of wheat may live in one of two ways—it may be planted and grow other grains, or it may be made into bread and nourish men. In both cases it must be destroyed before it is rendered useful. It must rot in the ground to sprout, or it must be ground to flour in order to make a loaf.

The apple-blossom's exquisite existence perishes so that the fruit may come into life.

All living things emerge from the womb of death.

Every dollar of profit is the spent life of some worker.

Life is an endless procession. All living things go down into death and come up again having received the strange baptism of new life. The plants, the flocks, the human creatures of today all move toward decay; a short time and everything that now is alive will be gone, to make way for the next order of living things.

Life is not a continuous stream; it is a pulsation, a coming and going.

You eat to sustain life, but every viand on your table represents destruction; your meats are slain animals, your fruits, vegetables, and cereals are slain plants. The purveyor of your feast is Death.

Old ideas and beliefs likewise perish that the new may draw sustenance from their dissolution.

From the death of the old credulities arises the beauty of faith. Out of decayed theologies come the new humanities. From dead monarchies are fed new democracies.

Astrology, necromancy, magic, and the like perished, and from their mould sprung up astronomy, psychology, biology, all the vigor of the young sciences.

The dominance of the Greek, the Roman, and the Hebrew had to pass, so that modern thought, organization, and ethical conviction might have life.

Competition must die that cooperation may live.

Privilege in its protean forms must be killed that justice and the common welfare be fattened upon its flesh.

It is of great concern to men how they may keep alive their institutions; it ought to occupy them still more how they can bury them. For in time every institution ceases to minister to life and becomes an instrument of death. The thing is to get rid of it with as little violence as possible when it ceases to serve men.

In time all sects must die, that religion may live; all nations must die, that humanity may live; all schools must die, that education may live; all people must die, that their children's children may live; all systems of truth, all statements of truth, all creeds must die, that truth may live and be ever green.

The universe is deciduous, not everlasting.

We die—forward!

"Thou fool, that which thou sowest is not quickened except it die."

THE LIMITATIONS OF SCIENCE

SCIENCE has done wonders, but it has its limitations.

In the days when Huxley and Tyndall were in their prime there was a feeling in the air that science was a new omnipotence that was about to solve all problems, cure all social ills, dispel all clouds of superstition, and bring the sunlight of truth and gladness of light upon earth.

The reaction could not fail to come. We have learned that science, too, is human.

The world is under an unpayable debt to the scientific spirit and the scientific method. They have done great things.

But there are other things, and the greatest things of all, that science cannot do.

For, after all, the eye of the scientist sees only appearances. The eye of the microscope, as a recent French essayist has said, is still only an eye, and sees only appearances.

Science recognizes only facts. But it is not facts that have the last word in life—it is the relations of human beings to those facts.

So it is always to the "seer," to the poet and prophet, the philosopher and the storyteller, that we must turn for our last adjustment.

When our facts are non-facts, when we base our preachment upon what is not true, of course we go astray. It is science that must lay our foundations, else the house is built on the sand and will not stand.

But science has been overpraised. It has made racing locomotives, huge steamships, telegraphic cables, and telephones. With these we have saved time and money, but we are no nearer the solution of the problem of what we shall do with the spare time we have gained or the excess wealth we have piled up.

Science has brought forth millionaires; it has not brought forth any word to make them a blessing and not a burden to the world.

It has enabled us to carry bodies ten times faster than in the age of Moses; it has not shown how to make the souls in those bodies nobler.

Is the mystery of love any clearer now than it was in the days of Abelard and Heloise?

Is death more understandable to the last mother who lost her baby than it was to Eve, sitting with dead Abel's head in her lap?

Are there modern formulas of friendship

more reliable than the instincts of Damon and Pythias?

Can the most learned savant of Harvard or the Sorbonne tell you anything new about how to starve the beast and nourish the angel in you, anything Marcus Aurelius or Paul of Tarsus had not told?

Has the most distinguished professor of sociology given us any new light on how human beings are to live in mutual helpfulness and peace, any light that goes beyond the beams cast by the pure ideals of Jesus of Nazareth?

Let us honor the scientist. He has abolished pests, increased comforts, banished the ghosts of ignorance, and taught us intellectual honesty.

But he has not healed the deep hurt of the world, and he never can. That takes another type of man.

THE NEED OF CHANGE IN GOVERNMENT

THE government ought to be changed. There never was a government that did not need changing. There never will be.

Certain reformers seem to imagine that if we could get a perfect government the ills of the nation would speedily be cured.

This is merely one form of that enthusiastic but mistaken dream to which in general mankind is prone; to wit, that we ourselves would be ideal if we only had ideal circumstances.

For government is but a circumstance, a part of our environment, one of the outward conditions to which we are subject; a very important one, to be sure.

But we might as well say, if we had an ideal family, or home, or town, or schools, or churches; for all these things mean simply ideal people, which you will probably never find.

We all have the perfect man, the faultless woman in our mind's eye; but we shall never see one with the eye of this flesh. The best we can do is to keep approximating to perfection as best we can.

The ideal government is simply that government where there is the maximum of order with the minimum of constraint.

We approach this only as individuals become by nature more orderly. As the citizen improves in self-control the control of government gradually disappears.

Absolutism and privilege are necessitated by ignorance; only intelligence and altruism can bring about pure democracy.

OUT OF IT

"I'M going to give up my job," said a young man to me the other day.

Now, his position was an enviable one. He had a good salary, and could hold his place during good behavior. He was fixed for life. He had a comfortable home with wife and baby. His work hours were short, allowing him plenty of leisure to amuse or to improve himself. His duties, while important, were such as he could easily discharge. The office, of which he was the head, practically ran itself, so well had he organized and systematized it.

A host of other young fellows looked on him with covetousness: He had arrived.

I asked him why he wanted to quit.

After reflecting a bit, to see if he could make himself understood, he said:

"Well, the trouble is, I'm out of it."

I did understand.

He was a real and an unspoiled soul, and to such to be out of it means to miss life.

What does it mean to be out of it?

It simply means not to be pitting one's self against hazard, or fate or luck or destiny, if you like, in gaining a livelihood.

To a normal, healthy man life is best when it is something of a game.

To have your living assured, to know that all you have to do to be provided for all your days is to be careful and not to be impudent to your employer, is something like shooting setting hens instead of flying ducks.

Very little good work in the world has been done by men in sinecures.

The great inventions somehow do not seem to come from endowed professors. The telegraph, the phonograph, the cinematograph, the sewing-machine, the steel-wool rubber, the automobile, the card-index system, the fountain-pen—what universities or technology institutes projected them?

What literary scholarship produced a Kipling, a Bernard Shaw, a Maupassant, a Wagner, or a Giotto?

And as for religion, St. Paul and Savonarola, Luther, Knox and Wesley, General Booth and Mrs. Eddy were only successful (I speak only of their results; I am no judge of their rightness) when they cut loose from all safety and risked ridicule, starvation, or worse.

Of all the people in the great business house, the man who is getting the most out of life is the man who is at the head, carrying the responsibility, not knowing whether tomorrow will bring loss or gain, putting his brain against all the chances of failure.

I wonder if socialists ever suspect that, if their fondest dreams should be realized and every man should have a good life-job, the fun of the thing would be taken out.

Of course, uncertainty of employment has its ugly side. But it is the ugly sides of things that make a man a man. Some souls are cowed by the whip of fortune; others are stung to courage and action.

To take away danger might save the weak, but it would ruin the strong.

We have often wondered why poets and artists and musicians are proverbially hungry; we do not realize the psychological connection between precariousness and good work.

To get the best work out of the highest types of minds you must throw them into the water and tell them to survive—or drown.

And this young man felt out of it, out of the big, bully man-struggle. He wanted to fight. He didn't want sugar-plums.

He, too, felt the call of the Spirit of Life, that ever says to the protected pets she loves and would make strong men of: "One thing thou lackest. Sell all thou hast and give to the poor, and come, follow me!"

CAPITAL

ALL progress is the accumulation of capital.

Any man's force is in what has been laid up for him, by others or by himself

We usually think that only money or things with money-value is capital.

But learning is capital. What is the young man at the medical or law school, or at the institute of technology, doing except getting a working capital of information?

The apprentice learning how to run a loco-motive, paint a house, manage an automo-bile, lay shingles, or make pastry is storing up skill-capital.

When he applies for a position he is asked

not only what he can do but what he has done; his experience is his capital.

A man's reputation is his moral capital.

A politician's record is his capital.

The soul has its capital; every triumph over an unworthy impulse, every successful struggle against an ignoble weakness, every deed of good and every resistance to the bad, enters as spiritual money, stocks, bonds, and negotiable values, into its bank of power.

Destroy all capital, or redistribute it, and the very first thing labor would do would be to begin anew to create it.

For the very purpose of labor is to make capital, as the business of bees is to make honey.

THE SQUIRREL

ONE summer morning, in Atlantic, Iowa, I rose early from an uncomfortable bed in the hotel, and went out into the little park that is in the central square of the town. There I sat under the trees beside a fountain and saw the dawn shimmer.

A little squirrel ran up to me, stopped, sat up, cocked his head, eyed me a minute and scampered away. Nothing could exceed the exquisiteness of his motion. His progress was a series of graceful undulations; he ran along the grass as a wave runs along the sea. Arched back and flowing tail were perfect curves.

What a bundle of finely wrought nerves

and muscles, what a little masterpiece of life from the hand of the most skilled of all artists, Nature!

And yet, I reflected, smitten by the plague of thought, to what purpose is all this workmanship? What was he made for? What will be his end? Some day, doubtless, to fall a prey to a cruel enemy, somewhere at last to lie and decay and give back all his marvellous machinery of fur and eye and throbbing heart to the rust of the earth and the gasses of the air. Beasts and birds, flowers and pretty girls, all this living jewelry, Nature wears but a day or so, and then throws it back into her laboratory to make new joy-things to deck herself withal.

For all that, every creature seems to be happy, except the human creature. He alone has the fatal gifts of memory and apprehension. He alone breaks the heart of the present between the upper and the nether mill-stones of the future and the past. The other animals drink the cup of joy when it is passed; our stomachs are dyspeptic with too much tomorrow and yesterday.

If the soul could only let itself sink into the perfect beauty and health and gladness of the present, it would taste the bliss of Nature's children.

Of course we must plan and we must regret. It is the backward look and forward look that make us great. And when occasion requires let us take up the burden of this tragedy. But as a habit of life, as an exercise for the better part of every day, let us sink into the wonder and beauty of what is, and not wear forever the suffocating garments of what was and what will be.

When death comes to the squirrel it is usually sudden death, which is the best kind.

He never feels it till he meets it, and the pang is not long.   It casts no shadow on his life.

And for us mortals it is not death, but "the valley of the shadow of death," that clouds life.

IT WON'T WORK

IT won't work, eh? You say it's all right to have ideals, but you've got to be practical in this world. Personal convictions are commendable, but in actual life one must trim, and accommodate, and compromise, to get along. It is well to be good and kind and generous, and to return good for evil, and turn the other cheek and all that, but really, you know, in this world one cannot possibly put such a program through. He would be eaten up.

So!

Yes, you continue, we must face facts. We must deal with stern realities. It is conditions that confront us, and not theories. We must live on earth, not among dreams.

76

Very well!

Let us stick to stubborn, hard, tough facts. Let us waste no time debating theories.

And let us ask:

1. Did you ever try the ideal life? Did you ever honestly, for a fair space of time, long enough to get results, test the plan of absolute intellectual honesty, altruism, and the principle of the Beatitudes?

Answer: The most of you have not. You simply THINK it won't work. You BELIEVE that you would be imposed upon, wronged, and devoured. It is YOU who are the theorist.

As a matter of fact, the majority of people don't know whether living the higher, finer, ideal life will work or not. They have never tried it.

2. How many persons do you know who do consistently and persistently try it?

Have you noted them carefully, if you have met any?

And if you have studied their cases, haven't you found that invariably they are cheerful, contented, happy, and strong in character?

Did it never occur to you, being a practical soul, that all this commonly accepted talk of "be good and you'll be lonesome," and "the Ten Commandments and the Sermon on the Mount are iridescent dreams," is sheer dogmatism, pure speculation, and rests on no facts whatever?

And what facts you do use are isolated, spasmodic experiments in idealism you have made, or have heard that others have made, here and there, and not any settled habit of life.

3. Also take a look at your samples—there are plenty of them—who are trying

the opposite program. The selfish, grasping, vindictive, vengeance-seeking, proud, shrewd, cunning, hard, cruel, pleasure-chasing crowd, eating and drinking to repletion, mad for new amusements, eager to be rich, famous, powerful—look at them, the world is full of them— are they full of the joy of life?

On the contrary, they are restless, unsatisfied, pessimistic, world-weary, bored, pitying their poor selves, and suspecting everybody else.

If you have so much "practical" common sense, why not use it? Why not get hold of a few facts and quit theorizing about something of which you have no actual knowledge?

It won't work, eh—to be good?

Perhaps not.   Try it and see.

MORALITY WRONG END TO

ANOTHER learned judge has advanced into the newspapers and declares ex cathedra that the telephone is corrupting the morals of our youth. Young Bill and Mary can talk much too easily, and the manufacture of "dates" is working overtime. Besides, telephoning greases the wheels of extravagance, since the housewife will not make hash out of the remnants of the roast when she can step to the 'phone and order a brand-new steak.

This sort of reasoning is not new. There never has been a step made in the improvement of human conditions but some moral monitor arose and pointed out that it would loosen the bonds of virtue.

Cities present greater advantages than the country for business, social life and amusement; and it is a gray-headed platitude that the city is far more dangerous to young people than the country.

Railways are more convenient than the one-hoss shay; but beware of them! for you might meet some one in the day coach who will speak to you.

Street cars are opportunities for promiscuous acquaintance; better walk; or still better, stay home.

Something ought to be done to protect innocence also from the United States Post-office!

The only really moral thing seems to be to lock your child up in the barn and feed him or her through a knot-hole.

This whole system of thought is based

upon the erroneous idea that it is a parent's chief duty to keep the child SAFE.

The truth, on the contrary, is that our main task is to train the child for intelligent liberty, to develop his sense of personal responsibility, and to equip him to take care of himself.

The needed lesson in life is to learn how to meet and deal with danger, and not how to avoid danger.

A judicious amount of authority is proper in parents, but if that authority is an end in itself, and if we only seek to teach the child to obey blindly, and do not train his own powers of resistance to evil, we do more harm than good.

Prohibition is right when a child cannot understand; but it is wrong even then when there is no effort to make him understand.

It is not Opportunity that threatens the

morals of youth; it is ignorance of mind and feebleness of character.

And there is only one way to insure the moral character and adequate intelligence of the people; and that is to teach ethics in the public schools, to train children there in honesty, cleanliness, and manhood, and to keep all the children during their nonage in school all the time.

Here, as I have pointed out often, is the running sore of our crime, pauperism, and all social evil—namely, our failure to care for the children, and of our thrusting of them, untrained, into the economic struggle.

Go back, teach, train, educate, develop, prevent; and let us have done with this medieval tinkering with telephones, theatres, and picnics to keep people decent!

SOMETHING TO LIVE FOR

LIVING is not much fun unless you have something to live for.

Bread is the staff of physical life; an aim is the staff of spiritual life.

Without some goal, some object toward which your thoughts, energies, and hopes bend, your life gets flabby. It also gets either cold and useless or fevered and poisonous.

By and by you hate yourself. And others are inclined to make it unanimous.

Man is not an independent animal. He is by nature dependent. He is essentially social. When he tries to go it alone, to be sufficient unto himself, he goes crazy.

There are some people who are unbalanced because they have taken up some absorbing ideal, such as religion, or patriotism, or money-making, or music. But for every one such there are twenty who are warped, morbid, and lopsided because they haven't any ideal at all.

"Hitch your wagon to a star," said the philosopher. If you don't hitch it to something it won't go.

What shall I live for? You can answer the question by another: What is worth dying for? When you've found the thing worth dying for you've found the thing worth living for.

There's more stimulus in a great aim than in any other intoxicant. It raises every faculty of you to the highest power. It clears your brain, fills your heart, and raises your happiness to flood tide.

Do you notice how happy the child in the house is when he is made to realize he has something to do; how happy the man when he feels that a family depends on him for support; how happy the woman when she sees that she is essential to some man's or children's happiness?

In all this horror of world war there is a kernel of joy. The bitter plant has borne at least one sweet fruit. Nations, and the millions in them, have found something to die for, hence to live for.

In a recent book, "From the Human End," by L. P. Jack, a distinguished Oxford professor, it is stated: "The war has brought to England a peace of mind such as she has not possessed for generations. That element of 'poise' in life which Matthew Arnold valued so highly has become an actual possession of millions in whom twelve months ago it was utterly lacking. It seems a strange phenomenon, and yet it is nothing more nor less than the peace of mind which comes to every man who, after tossing about among uncertainties, finds at last a mission, a cause to which he can devote himself, body and soul. At last he has something to live for, and though the living may be hard and costly he makes no complaint; all that is well repaid by the harmony that comes from the unitary aim of his life."

Thousands in the United States feel the same. To numberless young men the donning of the khaki means a certain ennoblement, an enrichment of life. By taking a great thought we have added a cubit to our stature.

A deep thrill is informing many a life that until now was full of self-contempt. The aimless young man is beginning to under-

stand the dignity and glory of a soul, who,
"If he be called upon to face
Some awful moment to which Heaven has
joined
Great issues, good or bad for humankind,
Is happy as a lover."

POMPEII, RAVENNA, AMERICA, AND
THE SOUL

THE two most interesting cities, in a certain way, in Italy are Pompeii and Ravenna. Pompeii is empty and desolate. Ravenna, once the capital of the country, is now a poor village, with a few huge churches and monuments of the past. From both the glory has departed. Life, that teemed so richly once in them, has turned to other channels. They lie asleep, forsaken, pathetic, abandoned.

So is our Past. I can look back upon Pompeiis and Ravennas in my own life. There are enthusiasms long burnt out; hours once full and fiery, but now empty sepulchres; plans, hopes, joys, sorrows, all stretching out along my path of years like the dismantled tombs along the Appian Way.

But—there is America, young, new, insurgent. Thank God! in me there is also an America. And there is where my soul lives, planning, creating, busy, hopeful, face to the front. So you and I, each of us is a little world, with our inner ruins and gray walls and crumbling idols; also with our inner Future, sunny and youthful forever.

If I should dwell among the things of my past I should be but an owl or a bat, infesting vacant and pensive solitudes.

But I am a Futurist, an American. Always before me are the Golden Days to come. From them I draw breath of life.

HERE'S TO YOUR GOOD HEALTH!

HERE'S to your good health!
A better toast cannot be drunk.

When we meet daily and give the usual greeting, "How are you?" we are asking the most important question in the world. It means, "What is your physical, bodily state today?" and implies that this is the main thing about you.

Time was when men flogged and starved the body to get the best results out of the soul. That was an error. We recognize now that the highest efficiency of a man comes from a perfect mind in a perfect body.

"Body for the sake of the soul," was Plato's motto.

Just what influence the body has on the mind we may not fully know. A scholium of Spinoza's was, "For what the body can do no one has hitherto determined."

The first duty of parents is to do what they can to insure good health for their children. For all the religion and intellect possible in a child can be spoiled by a bad liver.

How many "wicked" things are but the miasms of imperfect physical condition? The fretful, impatient, petulant, soured woman; the wayward, intractable child; the uncharitable, cranky, grouchy man, often but reap the results of the abused or neglected flesh.

It is not the devil, but dyspepsia, that makes us morbid and gloomy.

And much of the spiritual excellences come from good health:

"Spontaneous wisdom breathed by health,
Truth breathed by cheerfulness."

"Even the salt of the earth," writes John
MacCunn, in "The Making of Character,"
"may upon occasion be betrayed by nothing
more dignified than physical exhaustion or
irritability into judgments peevish, uncharitable, precipitate; and thereby be put to the
blush by their worldly neighbors in whom
the placid good health that goes with an
easy-going life has kept the balance true."

The time and attention given to physical
culture in our schools and colleges is wholly
inadequate. A few hours a week in the
gymnasium and an occasional lecture by the
director are absurd. Nothing but daily
practise and instruction can do justice to so
important a matter.

The overtraining of college athletics is as
bad as the neglect. The first duty of any

school is to graduate young human animals who are as fit as young panthers.

The declaration of Dr. Johnson, that illness makes a man a scoundrel, is doubtless an exaggeration. There have been many who have risen above disease and deformity into mental greatness and spiritual beauty.

But although poor health should make no one despair, yet the young person who fails to use every means to secure a sound body is guilty of the greatest folly.

If you want to be "free from the body," make it healthy. For as Rousseau said, "The weaker the body is the more it commands."

ISMS

PEOPLE do not dislike the practise of teetotalism, says Mr. Chesterton; it is the theory they object to. Neither do they dislike either vegetables or vegetarians.

"What is resented," he goes on to say, "is the religious atmosphere that goes with teetotalism. What is resented is the ethical atmosphere that goes with vegetarianism."

"What men resist," he says again, in one of his whimsical paradoxes, "What men resist, in short, in all these cases is not the moral conduct, but the morality. Nothing can be immoral except morality."

I am one of those who take Gilbert Chesterton seriously. He cannot fool me with the humor with which he coats his pills of wisdom so as to get the crowd to swallow them while laughing. He is not a literary vaudevillian. He is one of the most sane philosophers of our day.

In the above-quoted sentence he hits the nail squarely on the head. Morals are the salvation of men. Morality has been a chief factor in making men immoral.

I loathe an ISM. I like Americans, but most all of the Americanism I have seen is bumptious and vulgar. I believe in many of the ideas of the socialists, anarchists, and single-taxers; but socialism, anarchism, and single-taxism find me cold. Christians I regard as superior to pagans, yet what crime have been committed in the name of Christianity! Real Christians, for instance, would shun war and decline to torture their fellow creatures; yet these outrages have been cheerfully engaged in by Christianity

The trouble is that when you make an ISM you squeeze all the humanity out of the thing and get a purely intellectual product, a sect, cult, or system, a non-human affair; and what ceases to be human easily becomes diabolical upon occasion.

We become convinced of the truth of a certain idea; we want to advance the truth; we therefore form a party or movement; we are dazzled, humbugged, deceived by apparent rapid success. In reality we have stabbed the truth under the fifth rib.

Any truth or group of truths taken away from the human beings who hold them becomes half false and entirely dangerous.

Browning was wonderful; Browningism, the cult, is piffle. So are Bergsonism, and Emersonism, and Marxism.

So in morals. When a man has a moral conviction and rules his own life by it he is

4-7

like a green tree in a desert land unto his fellows; when he organizes and begins to impose his SYSTEM OF MORALITY upon others we flee him as the pest

The tyranny of a bad man is far more easily to be borne than moral tyranny. For the tyranny of the wicked is usually entirely personal, while that of the moral becomes a perfected Juggernaut car, utterly without bowels of mercy.

And why cannot a man speak forth the truths he sees here and there without somebody running up to him and clapping a LABEL on him?

When I meet a deeply moral man, who keeps his mouth shut and does not try to uplift me, I am unlifted, I am made more moral by his presence; when the professional uplifters get after me with their systems of morality I have a strong desire to rob a bank.

THE HEALING POWER OF HOUSE-
KEEPING

NO, said Emily, I don't board, and I
don't live in a hotel. I keep house.
I have a little flat of four rooms. It's full
of my own junk. Poor stuff, perhaps, but
mine own.

Every piece of furniture in it is a friend
of mine. I love my kitchen table, my chaf-
ing-dish, my knives and spoons, my alumi-
num sauce-pan, and my tea-pot.

There's not an article in my home that is
not hand-picked. I went to the stores my-
self and bought. I love to go shopping about
once a month or so. You know I am a literary worker. And to such there is no soul-
balm like a department store.

Look at that linen lunch-cloth. I got it last week. Six seventy-five. Isn't it lovely? I walked miles of aisles and dug through mountains of cloth to find it. There at last it was, mine from the foundation of the world, waiting for me. See how happy it is. I love things like some other old maids love cats and dogs.

I love a home. I don't particularly want a husband, and, for that matter, none has particularly wanted me. So we're both pleased. And I don't want children. I just want a home, a place of my own. I want my own darling rocking-chair, and mahogany lamp, and gilt mirror, and Chinese rug, and my vases and everything.

I like to dust them, and arrange them in new positions, and sit and look at them. Isn't that a darling angel water-pitcher and thermos bottle combined? It has sung esthetic beauty to my soul that is worth many times over the eight dollars I paid for it.

There's a healing power in housekeeping. When I come home tired and unravelled you can't imagine the sweet influence of that dictionary-holder and that bookcase upon my spirit.

And then to go out into the kitchen and make me an omelet with cheese, and some French toast—dipped in egg and milk, you know, and fried in lots of butter till it's crisp, and a cup of coffee in my glass percolator, and broil a slice or two of bacon, and have a little cherry preserves for dessert— why, by the time I've done all that, and eaten, and put away the things, I feel that my wearied soul has nested like a bird that has been dodging hawks and cats and hunters all day.

Things are such a blessing. They are such a refuge from the stress of ideas and people.

They are calm. They have such poise. They are dependable; they stay put.

I love my bed, and it loves me, and is good to me. My bathroom is a white dream. My piano—but why run on?

I say there's a healing power in housekeeping. When I'm a little tired I cook. When I'm worried I sweep. When I'm distressed I shop. And when I feel a spell of sickness coming on I clean house.

WHERE TO TAKE HOLD

THE place to take hold is Here.

Right Here.

And the time to begin is Now.

Right Now.

If you don't know how to go at it right, go at it wrong, but go at it.

All the worth-while things of this life are difficult. Nothing's easy but slumping.

Most of the problems that affect your happiness are complicated.

And the way to perform a difficult and complicated task is to go to it—somehow.

For you learn by trying.

Life is an Art, not a Science. It is mastered by experiment, and patience, and infi-

nite beginnings again. Nobody in the world
can learn just what to do before he does it;
I mean in the way of living and getting
along.

If you have to see a man, and dread the
interview, because he is an impossible fellow and will make things as hard for you
as he can, go right away and get it over
with.

If your desk is cluttered with a dozen
half-finished matters, clean it up now. De-
cide. Act.

If you owe money, pay it. If you cannot pay it, make the best arrangements you
can with your creditor now. Don't evade
and equivocate. Don't dawdle.

If you have a lesson to learn at school,
and it looks formidable, and you don't see
how you can possibly master it by tomorrow's class, go at it, learn a little of it now.

get what you can of it, only don't wait for some miracle to happen.

If you have a bad habit that is throttling you, take hold now. You must conquer it some time, and every day you delay your fight your enemy grows stronger.

If you want to save money and get a little ahead, put a portion of what you have now in the savings-bank. Nothing is finished that was never begun.

If you really want to be charitable and help your fellow-man, give of what you now possess.

If you are not helpful with a dollar only in your pocket, you would not be if you had a million.

Do it now.

What you are going to do some day may be a sickly dream. It's what you do today that means something.

The only theory that is of any value is the one that gets into your fingers right now.

The only Creed that will save your soul is the one that flushes your heart and thought and speech and deed now.

The place to take hold is Here.

THE BODY AND THE AUTOMOBILE

IF I were young again, said the old man,
I'd—but there! What's the use? As
soon as a man accumulates sense enough to
know how to live he has to die.

But I was just thinking. There's my automobile. I hire a chauffeur to take care
of it. He watches it like William J. Burns.
He is always washing it, polishing it, tight-
ening a screw here and regulating a valve
there, nosing around under the hood—even
when we're riding he listens to its purr as a
doctor listens to a man's heart.

Why do I have this piece of machinery so
looked after? Because I want to get all
the use out of it there is in it.

Well, if I were twenty-one I'd take as good care of my body as I do of my automobile. And for the same reason—to get a hundred per cent. efficiency and fun out of it. The body is the most important machine a man has, and certainly he's a fool to neglect it, as I've neglected mine, I'm sorry to say.

I'd watch what I put into it, for one thing. I'd cut out eating as a form of diversion. I'd reduce it to the same level as putting gasoline into the motor tank—something done to make the thing go, not something done for the fun of doing it.

I'd learn all about these calories—never heard of 'em till after I was fifty—and food values, and so on, and I'd take in just exactly what I needed to keep my body strong, my mind clear, and my disposition good. I wouldn't pour a lot of meat and pastry and booze into my gasoline-tank just because other fools around me were doing it.

There are other ways of getting enjoyment out of a motor than by putting garbage into the gas-tank.

Once or twice a year, also, I'd have my works overhauled by experts. I'd go to some institution where they practise science and not quackery, and be looked over from head to toe.

Twice a year I'd have my teeth examined. I waited till they hurt—and now look at me. Everybody has to take medicine some time, and the best kind is preventive medicine.

And I'd have my heart tested, and my urine analyzed, and my blood-pressure ascertained, and all the rest of the things they've been doing to me of late—I'd have them all done beforehand. I don't wait till my automobile breaks down or blows up. I see to it that it's in good trim all the time.

It's queer how a man goes along abusing his body, loading it up with waste, letting it get rusty and rattly—what if he did that with his two-thousand-dollar car? What if he left that out in the rain, and let the carburetor get dirty and the cylinders full of carbon, and paid no attention to it generally? Wouldn't he be a fool?

Well, he's fooler when he doesn't keep his body in order. For his body's more than a two-million-dollar machine, and has more to do with his happiness or misery than any contraption of steel and brass.

Yes, sir; if I were young again I'd take as good care of my body as I do of my automobile.

COLLEGES AND AUTOMOBILES

"I DON'T know what to do with my boys. They are through high-school, ready for college, and I have about made up my mind that they shall not go to college."

It was a gentleman of culture, of means, and of some standing in the professional world who was speaking. He was an old friend of mine; we were lunching together, with a third man.

"Modern schools, and particularly modern universities, are medieval hang-overs. In an age of progress they are the most stupidly reactionary of all our institutions. They are advanced enough in some things; in fact, they are advanced in everything—except in education.

111

"They have not the first notion of equipping a boy for life.

"They can develop a schoolmaster, an engineer, or an expert of one kind or another, but they cannot develop a well rounded human being.

"I don't know why I should send my sons to four years of the dark ages as to their studies, and four years of absolutely vicious and demoralizing social life as to their leisure hours.

"I think I shall put them to work and have them take up the Chautauqua course in their spare time.

"It would seem that in this era of mad prosperity and its attendant materialism and low ideals the university should be the place where the youth could be shown the real and serious facts of life, where there could be plain living a..d high thinking, where souls could be shaped into sterling character and the gentle love of letters be instilled.

"But what do you find? Look here at what Dr. Arthur G. Webster of Clark University says."

He showed me an article in a newspaper wherein were these strictures by Dr. Webster:

"The result of our prosperity is swollen fortunes, the automobile classes, the pursuit of pleasure, the exaggeration of dancing, the lack of interest in all things that cannot be measured by the yardstick of business success.

"About all that people want to know about now are automobiles, dancing, movies, and baseball.

"Show me a boy who is interested in arithmetic, and I will show you a hundred interested in the newest self-starting gear.

4-8

"The automobile, while of course not immoral itself, seems to lend itself eagerly to every species of crime, from that of the Paris apache to that of the Harvard loafer.

"It is no secret that there are loafers at Harvard. There are too many automobiles, too much 'gold coast' and too much of the outside activities. Harvard is, however, no worse than Yale, Princeton, or any of the colleges of the Atlantic seaboard. What is true of one is true of all.

"The big colleges are fast becoming known by their athletic achievements rather than their positions as educational centres. Their graduates care little for learning in any form. Recently dozens of classes held reunions and whooped up for dear old Harvard. In these class reunions if anybody endeavored to make a speech pertaining to learning he would be howled down.

"The most discouraging fact in connection with American education is the lack of interest in it, and the ignorance regarding it among educated men."

"But," said the gentleman with side whiskers, who made the third of our party, "but, that is doubtless exaggerated. There is something to be said on the other side."

"There is always something to be said on the other side of anything that's endowed for a million or so," said my friend.

THE SECOND-TERMER

IT is the rule of courts pretty generally throughout civilization to give second-termers a longer prison sentence than first offenders. When I was on the State Parole Board in Illinois I found an ironclad precedent that, while the convict was usually paroled at the end of a year if it was his first term, he was remanded back to the penitentiary for an extra year for every term he had served before in any penitentiary.

The object of this procedure seems plain. It is to make the law a terror to the professional crook. It is to make a criminal fearful of breaking the law twice.

Upon the premises the reasoning is good.

But the premises are wrong. It is assumed that crime can be cured by punishment, which is untrue.

Men may commit their first offense because of the frailty of perversion of human nature. Men are made confirmed criminals, are permanently set in evil, and become life members of the criminal class by prisons. The penitentiary is a device for developing ordinary wickedness and making it practically incurable.

When a man breaks the law and becomes a menace to society, common sense would indicate that the state segregate him and endeavor to correct his evil tendency, or, failing in that, keep him where he can do no harm.

As a matter of fact, when one is guilty of a crime, instead of curing him or attempting to cure him, so that he will no more be dangerous, we place him in an institution where his natural criminality is increased, his self-respect, which alone can preserve him, broken down, and he is treated in such a way as daily and hourly to remind him that he is viler than others, and that there is no good in him.

In other words, we do our best to make of him a hopeless offender. Then when he is turned loose with a cheap suit of clothes and five dollars, the police dog him, detectives watch him, and upon the least suspicion he is haled into court, where, finding he is an ex-convict, no mercy is shown him.

The state punishes him for its own failure, for its own crime.

The state systematically crushes the manhood out of him and then punishes him for its own work.

The whole penitentiary idea is rotten.

The very atmosphere of state prisons is laden with that despair that turns human beings into werewolves.

There is plenty of intelligence and scientific truth in the twentieth century, and these ought to be used in the treatment of moral defectives.

From a somewhat extensive experience I would say that five-sixths of the convicts sent to penitentiaries might be restored to useful citizenship if they were put somewhere where they would be handled as human beings, their self-respect restored, and their perverted natures treated as sensibly as physicians treat diseased bodies.

And the second-termer ought to have even more care than a first-termer.

THE DEMAND FOR PREACHING

PEOPLE want preaching.

That statement is made in defiance of the common notion to the contrary.

People are deserting the churches not because they don't like preaching, but because they don't get it.

Men and women are now, as they always have been since they emerged from animalism, and as they always will be till the end of time, more deeply interested in the problems of death, of the meaning of life, of conscience, of sorrow, of peace, of God and immortality, than they are in making money, playing baseball, and cracking jokes.

They may not seem so, but they are. The

civilized man of today conceals his deepest concerns.

People want to know how to be true, happy, brave, good, and loving.

Anybody that will talk or write on these themes, and do so in plain English, and in a human way, and with genuine sincerity, and without some ulterior motive or selfish scheme up his sleeve, will find an audience; that is, of course, provided he is not in an organization that chokes to death all his effort.

There should be more books of plain moral instruction. Essays as a rule are flippant and purposely trivial. It is the utter uselessness of the essay literature that has killed it.

But abandon posing and fine writing and speak clear words right at the hearts of men and they will respond.

This is a day when story-telling is over-worked. As a consequence the average story is poor. Magazines have become as conventional as pulpits. They print nothing except that which conforms to certain established types. Originality and virility languish.

There is a vast virgin field for gifted writers upon life, its philosophy and its sanctities.

The numberless unchurched masses are hungry for the Word now, as they always have been. Only it must be disinfected from medievalism. It must be real and ring true.

Even if people will not admit they care about being good, they want their children to be good.

Tell us, say the dumb masses, if there be a way how to be at peace with the unknown without stultifying the intelligence;

how to cull the joy of love and escape the
thorn of lust; how to be reverent and not
bigoted; how to have content and not lose
ambition; how to be patient and not a
drudge; how to be clean and sweet and not
a prude and characterless; how to be great
and not vain; how to meet death with joy,
but not in a silly delusion.

The great bulk of the people today are
better than they have ever been before in
the world.

America is seething with moral sap.

Let the leaders emerge from their medievalism and speak plain words of heart and
fire and human interest to us, and we will
listen.

CATCH-PHRASES

"MAN shall not live by bread alone, but principally by catch-phrases," said Robert Louis Stevenson.

It is troublesome to think. The catch-phrase is ready-made thought. Most people much prefer it to their own.

This, of course, does not refer to you and me, but to the other fellows.

Multitudes live and die in sweet faith in a darling catch-phrase that is not true at all, or, what is worse, is half-true.

Most proverbs are but canned intellectual bromide. There are times, especially in life's crises, when the opposite of the old proverb, whatever it be that the wiseacres throw at you, is truer than the proverb itself.

Here are a few whiskered old flat ones I have met within the last few days. Some of them were handed me by ladies; some I saw wandering down newspaper columns, some lay safely asleep in books.

"You can get nothing done without organization." The fact is that while, for a certain kind of efficiency organization, the institution is a good thing, there are certain other desirable results which organized effort absolutely prevents. For instance, there is a deal to be said on the other side, when it comes to the permanent value of the educational, the charitable, and the ecclesiastical institution.

"The Weaker Sex." A very dangerously truthful delusion. The man who gets the obsession that he is stronger than a woman usually comes to grief.

"To abate these crimes we need severer

punishments." The idea that "the punishment should fit the crime," and that thereby crime will be estopped, belongs to the half-brute stage of civilization. Did you ever reflect that the root-difference between the New Testament and the Old consists in the abandonment of the punishment error? "An eye for an eye" was replaced by "turn the other cheek."

"Pure democracy consists in letting the people vote for every official and every measure." Quite the contrary. To overwhelm the citizen with responsibility for a mass of administrative detail is to throw, automatically, the government into the hands of the grafters. In an effective democracy the citizens vote for as few men and things as possible.

"We should all try to do good to others, to help and to uplift them." I think it was

Thoreau who said that if he saw one coming with the intent to do him good he would take to his heels. The truth is that the most altruistic thing a man can do is to do justice himself, and to establish just conditions upon the earth. The merchant or manufacturer who supplies work for a hundred heads of families is greater in the Kingdom of Heaven than the rich man who gives charity to a thousand.

"Senators are all owned by Big Business; newspapers are all controlled from the business office; preachers are all afraid of the pew-renters; and all women are frail. There is no chance for an absolutely honest man. Graft, forwardness, deception, and pull gain all the prizes." The man who believes these things, the sooner he is nicely tucked under the sod the better for him and for us all. Senators, editors, priests, and women are

mostly human, about as you and I. Most
people would rather be decent and straight
than not, simply because it is much more
comfortable.

"To err is human." It is not to err that
is peculiar to human beings. Beasts err also.
That which is distinctly human is to realize
that one has erred and to be sorry for it.

So it goes. Don't do your thinking in
prepared pills. Don't eat intellectual canned
goods exclusively.

THE STENOGRAPHER

SHE sits in the corner by the window and most of the time is clicking away at her machine. Sometimes she is reading a book, when work is slack, or may be seen gazing wistfully out of the window. She is thinking of her world, all so differently staged and peopled from this world of yours which she intersects.

You say, "Take this, please," and she comes with her notebook, slips her pencil from her back hair, and adjusts herself to record your words.

She tries to be a mere machine, which is the instinctive defense of womanly dignity. Her master-thought is to maintain her function of a recording instrument, to cover up her soul by routine; she is to be no more than a phonograph and a mechanism to type letters, arrange papers, and keep books.

She never succeeds. She is a human being. The soul keeps cropping out. Human flowers spring here and there through the oaken staves of her assumed restraint.

She is a woman. You are a man. You sit in the same room, or in adjoining rooms for six hours or so a day. It is impossible that no waves of man-woman electricity should pass.

Hers is the difficult task. She must be agreeable enough to hold her job. She must be coldly impersonal enough to keep the male creature at the proper distance.

She is usually a brave soul, and wise. She has no chaperon, and no conventions of society for walls to protect her. She must mingle with men, impersonally as men meet each other, yet she must remain her maidenly self.

She knows your business, and to a degree your domestic secrets, yet she must seem not to know. She knows your petulancies, tempers, and weaknesses. She knows better than your left hand the charities your right hand performs. She has seen your little meanness, glimpsed your courage and honor, and spied out more of your inner nature perhaps than your wife or your nearest friend has been privileged to perceive.

Yet to you she must remain a little stranger, an intimate stranger, a girl yet an equal, drawing her own conclusions yet never presuming to ask an explanation as to what you do, a woman with a man's relation to you, a woman who must not talk, a sharer of the most important privacies of your business who must forget all she hears, your comrade for six hours a day and a mere acquaintance outside of the office.

Yet she is a woman and has pervaded your place. She subtly affects your correspondence, she curbs the loose tongues of your callers, she continually reminds you that you are a gentleman; and if she be an honest and true little woman, and most stenographers are that, she indirectly moulds you in forty ways, much more than you admit; and your debt to her cannot be wholly measured in dollars and cents.

REMNANTS OF PAGANISM

"OBSERVE not," said Saint Eloy, of the seventh century, in a famous sermon, warning his flock against the seductions of Paganism, "Observe not the sacrilegious customs of the heathen, nor consult their charlatans, seers, sorcerers or magicians; observe not their augurs or sneezers, and when upon the road pay not heed to the songs of birds."

"Let no Christian observe a lucky day for leaving home or returning. Let none pay attention to the phase of the moon when he undertakes a work. Let none light torches and make vows at old temples, rocks, groves, paddocks, or crossways; let none make a holiday of Thursday; let none suspend from the neck of man or other animal phylacteries, even if offered by clerks and called sacred, under pretext that they contain passages of Scripture; let none presume to make lustrations, nor enchant herbs, nor cause his flock to pass through the hole of a tree or a ditch of the earth, which is in some sort to consecrate them to the devil.

"Let no woman wear amber at her neck; let none howl during an eclipse of the moon; let none believe in fate, fortune, or horoscope.

"In case of sickness, seek not the enchanters, diviners, sorcerers, or soothsayers. Consult not charms at springs, trees, or forks of the road. But let the fountains be, and cut down the trees they call sacred."

In its time the sermon was a very serious matter, a heavy blast of artillery against the wiles of superstition. Today what strange deeps it stirs in us!

We are a little civilized and Christian at the top, but in the dark reaches of the heart exist still what jungles of unacknowledged belief!

How we secretly fear Fridays and thir-teens, and note bad signs and runs of luck! Can we keep down the little shiver when some ignorant gypsy tells us that there will be a death in the family within a year?

We have driven the fairies and spooks and silly credulities from our cerebellum, but they linger in the spine.

After all our science the world we live in and the very soul itself are fringed with mystery. We have explored the globe, even Central America and the two Poles, but there are in ourselves vast forests, fearsome mountain peaks, unplumbed caverns, uncrossed deserts, and oceans over which no Columbus has ever sailed.

The little gods of other days still haunt us. All around our Science is the wide ocean of Nescience. Pale ghosts of forgotten faiths lurk in the back rooms of the brain. Wayward instincts underlie the will.

Often the abandoned Paganism of our forefathers moves within us; and for all the efforts of good Saint Eloy to plant the cross upon the unknown, will move and linger many a generation to come; and—it is not without its charm.

COCK-SURENESS

IT is as bad to be too cock-sure of things as it is to be a doubter. Somewhere between these two extremes you want to build your house.

The great point is, to be sure enough of a thing, so as to be able to use it, to live by it, to take it as a rule of conduct or a basis of morals, and at the same time to admit that you may be mistaken, and therefore, to be open to conviction.

There are many truths good enough to work with in the world, that cannot be declared absolutely indubitable. In fact the most vital and necessary truths are precisely the ones that are essentially dubitable. You must eat, and you don't know the food is not poison; you must sleep, yet you don't know an earthquake will not tumble your house down on you; you must love, and you never know absolutely, you can only believe, that love is returned; you must obey God, and live for an immortal life, yet no man has seen God, at any time, and none has returned from the shades beyond the grave. The higher, nobler, and more worthy a man's life, the more it is woven of questionable, debatable material.

This we find out when we grow old. When we are young we are cock-sure. "Every new idea," says Castelar, "tends to make itself absolute, tends to cancel all limits, to break over all opposition to believe itself to be the only idea fit to live in the universe, and sufficient to solve all problems."

WHAT DID WE GET FOR OUR MONEY?

I SAT down at the club the other day and along came my friend the single-taxer. I like single-taxers. They rank with Christian Scientists and Socialists as our most enthusiastic believers, and in "these days of down-pulling and disbelief," to use Carlyle's phrase, it is refreshing to meet a man that believes hard. My own temper of mind being somewhat critical and inclined to question, I look with envy upon men of militant positivity. It's a good thing somebody is sure of something.

He held me in some interesting conversation which I herewith pass on to those more learned and equipped in economics than I.

"We've just paid twenty-five million dollars for the Danish West India islands," he said. "What did we get for our money?"

"Why, we got the islands, I suppose."

"We did, did we? Who's we?"

"Why, the people of the United States."

"Not at all. Those islands belong to a few landowners. They owned them when they were Danish. They own 'em now they are American. Just got a different colored flag, that's all."

"Well, there's something in that."

"Yes, sir. One of those islands, St. Croix, is as large as Manhattan Island, and it is owned entirely by three men. There are 25,000 people on St. Croix engaged in raising sugar-cane. For the privilege of living and working there they must give the three owners the greater part of the wealth they produce, just as the people on Manhattan Island must give the Astors and a few other families a big part of their earnings for the privilege of living there.

"Now that the United States has paid $25,000,000 for the power to govern the islands, it should do one of two things: It should either empower the 25,000 people who live on St. Croix to take for common use the rental value of the islands they live on, and should empower the people of the two other islands to do the same thing, or it should take the rental value itself and use the money for the benefit of the islanders. That is one way that we can get value in return for the $25,000,000 spent. Until we do take this rental value for public use, not one cent should be taken in taxation from the laborers who are producing wealth on the islands."

I repeated this conversation to a college

professor and bitterly opposed to single tax. He said:

"Stuff and nonsense!"

I was glad to hear this convincing refutation of the single-taxer's screed. I knew there must be some answer to his specious arguments, of course, but I couldn't think what it was.

SOMEBODY IS FOLLOWING YOU

SOMEBODY is following you.

Somebody sees your footprints in the sand and is unconsciously going your way.

Somebody is catching a glimpse of you as you thread your way through life's mysterious woods, and is coming after you, perhaps merely because he knows no better direction to take.

Thackeray said that no Irishman was so poor that he did not have a still poorer Irishman living at his expense. And nobody is so insignificant and commonplace that he does not determine by his example the life of some one else.

We are fond of underrating ourselves, to

escape responsibility. But the fatal power
of leading others is unescapable. They follow us whether we will or no, and often the
more persistently in such measure as we
have no wish to be followed.

For the examples most doggedly imitated
are of those who do not set themselves up
as examples.

When a man cries, "Do not as I do," then
his manners take strongest hold on us.

It is not the great models of conduct and
piety that grasp us; it is the little every-day
models of negligence.

The boy swears and goes dirty to be like
Huck Finn. The little girl melts into the
mould of the silly and simpering miss. The
youth drinks because others drink.

People do things because others do, more
than for any other reason.

This is the strange force of crowds, where

we are swept along by the cumulative power of example to do what in our sober judgment we would never have done.

A little of this pulling power rests in every one of us. No matter how small and inconsiderable a person you seem to yourself to be, some one is being led by you by the invisible towlines that reach out from you to him.

No soul walks alone.

No act of self-restraint or of petulance is without an echo in some one.

Down the ways of life you walk at the head of some sort of a procession. Dimly and instinctively they follow you.

Unconsciously, even more than consciously, you are making this world a better or a worse place, you are adding to its pile of happiness or its heap of misery, you are shedding light or spreading gloom.

You cannot help it so long as you live.

When the final books are balanced it is your "little nameless unremembered acts" that will weigh most.

EIGHTEEN

A ND they are going to take the eighteen-
year-old boys into the army, said the
big hardware-dealer, as we sat at lunch in a
downtown restaurant.

That's the thing that's brought the war
home to our house. Have you got an eight-
een-year-old in your family? Well, we
have in ours. He's the only kid we've got.
Gosh! it seems like yesterday that he was
sitting up to the table in his high chair and
eating his meals with a spoon and pusher.
His mother still tucks him in bed and wor-
ries about his underwear.

Eighteen! Tom! Gee! I was looking
at him yesterday as he was playing tennis

in the yard. I thought of the things that fill his mind; the different makes of tennis rackets, and breeds of pups, and steps in a dance, and getting initiated in the Kappa Gammas, and the trick they played on Buster Lewis, and what a peach the new girl is that's visiting Sue Maynard, and his first dress-suit. Him? War? Gosh!

He couldn't go into any business. He's too kiddy to hold down a regular job; but he's going out to take up the most serious business in the world.

I paid my income tax, and forty other taxes, and ate bran, and did without meat, and bought Liberty Bonds and War Stamps, and declaimed over the war news in the papers, and thought I was a hundred-per-cent. patriot. But I tell you, this war never got under my skin till they handed me this wallop. Tom!

Why he's just a kid. He doesn't know enough to......The hardware man gave a big gulp.

The worst thing about it is his mother. She isn't raising Cain over it, and crying and taking on. No. It wouldn't be so bad if she did that. She's taking her medicine. But the way she does it she scares me. She just tiptoes around the house as if there were a funeral. And the way she smiles and tries to act cheerful is enough to break your heart.

The other night she woke me up and said, "Do you mind if I talk a little?" and caught my hand tight. Of course I said: "Sure not. What is it, Honey?"

And she said, "Don't you remember when I took him to the barber-shop and had his curls cut off?"

"Yes. I was mad, too, when I came home and saw his little head all cropped."

"And his first breeches? Wasn't he proud, though?"

"Sure!"

"I have....I have....got those breeches yet. They're in the bottom drawer of the bureau in the spare room."

"Have you?" I couldn't think of anything else to say.

"And," she went on after awhile, "I don't believe I can stand it!" And she put her arm over me and sobbed herself to sleep.

Tom came in next day, all excited and full of war. He had borrowed a military hat, and was saluting all over the place. His eyes snapped and his face was aglow. You could see it was a grand lark for him. I suppose that's what makes boys good soldiers. They don't know enough to get scared.

So he's going. Tom!

Well, Mr. Baker can have him, and feed him to the Hun. It's our bit, and we'll do it. But don't imagine that it doesn't hurt. I'd be glad to give my old carcass instead, only they wouldn't take it.

But Mother hung a brand-new flag up in the dining-room yesterday, and when I noticed it, she said, kinda soft, as she does when she's terribly in earnest:

"We're going to love that flag as we never did before."

"Yes," I said, "and we're only one of thousands."

"Thousands and thousands. . . . But I feel differently about it now. I'm glad. Away down in my heart I think I'm happier than I've ever been in my life. I can't describe it. It's something like religion. I'm just glad to feel that I'm doing the very, very hardest thing in the world for my country."

She smiled, but a couple of tears rolled down her face.

Well, that's the way the war has come home to us.

Tom! My God, think of it! Eighteen!

PAN

I SAW him. I did not see him. A caper, a whisk, and some creature vanished in the leafage before my eye could catch it. Was it Pan? or a squirrel? or a shy bird?

I sat long in the woods, and very still, which is the only way to see the little people. After a while they came out, peeping all furtive, looking steadily at me with their beady eyes, then they would dart forward, and squat and eye me again.

They were all so silent, so velvet-footed, so alert. They ate with extreme suspicion, making hurried nibbles and quickly looking around again for danger. The very spirit of danger seemed everywhere. The little creatures were all guarding their lives.

Only the birds were not quiet. They screamed and chattered and whistled snatches of wayward tune as they sped with a whir of wings from bough to bough.

Slowly the shadows moved, the sunlight wove its lacework on the ground, the trees bowed and waved in the breeze. The woodsy silence flecked with bird-notes enveloped me. My soul sank into the green deeps.

What was that? A grinning face, a hirsute leg, or merely some composition of the leaves? I must be still, still as this old log on which I sit, immovable as Nature's self, if I would see Pan.

And you cannot see him if you look directly at him. You must get him out of the tail of your eye. All the old gods are glimpsed, not seen. For the little divinities of earth are matters of half-knowledge, not knowledge.

And they are to be sensed, not understood. Such crudities as intellect, reason, and logic cannot find them. Your soul must sink into "a wise passiveness" and thrust its timorous antennæ out.

So I found Pan. Not that I saw him with mental eyes. But I heard him whistling in the distance, though it might have been a bird, and whispering above me, though another might have said it was the tree-tops, and I caught his dim lowings and wisp-like flutings and surreptitious scamperings.

And by and by he came to me and told me all about life, and the myriad lives, and what the stuttering water said in the brook, and many secrets of "that vast nescience upon which science floats as a superficial film."

Then I took leaves and made a wreath and put it on my head, and my lover did likewise, and we intoned John Keats' hymn to Pan, and the meaning of it fell back upon us as a violet mist, and our hearts were enlarged, and a little afraid, and not happy, but as it were trembling upon the brink of a vast happiness that we could not be simple enough to understand, because we were only human. "Strange ministrant of unimagined sounds That come a swooning over hollow grounds, And wither drearily on barren moors, Dread opener of the mysterious doors That lead to universal knowledge, see, Great son of Dryope, Us that have come to pay our vows With leaves about our brows."

THE MODERN CRAZE FOR BEAUTY

"POOR thing!" wrote a woman to me, speaking of a young girl in whom we were both interested, a girl of talent and spirit and little money. "Poor thing! I feel sorry for her. She so loves pretty things, and I don't see where she is going to get them."

The poor thing in question had merely the spirit of her age. One of the strongest traits of the present younger generation is a fierce craving for beauty.

People want to be beautiful as they never longed for personal charm before. I cannot believe our great-grandparents felt the chagrin of an unattractive face as keenly as our children feel it.

The world today wants beautiful things
more than the world of yesterday. Not
only do women crave pretty clothes and furniture and back yards, but men wish more
beauty in the office and the workshop.

You do not understand this in the least
if you interpret it to mean merely a lust for
luxury, a spendthrift craze for show. It is
not that, it is the forthputting of an inde-
structible human instinct, which has been
long repressed by other forces and is now
asserting itself.

The nineteenth century was the most wonderful of all the forty centuries or so humanity has existed. It was marked by the
advance of science, the rapid development
of democracy, the final emancipation from
hierarchy, the decay of war, the unprece-
dented growth of commercialism, and the
accumulation of wealth.

It was also probably the ugliest century since the Stone Age.

The Greeks carried the expression of beauty very far. Roman life may have been cruel, but it was not unpleasing to the eye in its costumes and buildings, and medievalism was as picturesque as it was dirty. But the nineteenth century was just plain ugly the world over.

The mind of man cannot conceive an artistically more absurd dress than a silk hat, dress suit, and patent-leather shoes, wherein the man arrays himself when he wants to be at his best.

Of women's attire I shall say nothing, being a prudent man, and married.

All modern cities are utterly inartistic, all villages violate every canon of good taste; and not content with that, we daub the landscape with hideous billboards.

Now, human nature cannot endure this. It cannot go on indefinitely making money, amassing facts, and merely getting on. It has beauty hunger in it.

Slowly that beauty hunger is beginning to show itself.

We are getting more beautiful chairs, tables, houses, streets, and bric-à-brac.

The progress is painfully slow and difficult to discern, but there is progress.

When the great spirit of democracy steadies itself and gets over its youthful crudities and excesses, it will express its private and public life in clothes, dwellings, and cities far more beautifully than the Greek, Roman, or medieval spirit ever did, because it is intrinsically a far more beautiful spirit than theirs.